KW-043-760

Handbook on Alcoholism for Health Professionals

Dr Ludwig Bieder
MD FRACP

*Physician in Charge, Detoxication and Clinical Assessment Unit,
Palmerston North Hospital, New Zealand*

Dr John O'Hagan
FRACP FRCP(Edin) MRNZCGP

*Physician, The Princess Margaret Hospital, Christchurch
Associate Dean for Postgraduate Affairs,
Christchurch Clinical School of Medicine, New Zealand*

Dr Edwin Whiteside
MB ChB BSc Dip Chem Dep (Toronto)

*Physician to the Alcohol and Drug Centre, Wellington Hospital
and The Bridge Programme, Wellington, New Zealand*

Edited by
Dr Alex Paton

*Regional Postgraduate Dean, British Postgraduate Medical Federation
University of London, United Kingdom*

William Heinemann Medical Books Ltd
London

616.86

BIE

First published in New Zealand in 1982 by the
Alcoholic Liquor Advisory Council as the
Handbook on Alcoholism for Medical Practitioners

Adapted and published in Great Britain in 1985 by
William Heinemann Medical Books Ltd, 23 Bedford Square,
London WC1B 3HH

© William Heinemann Medical Books Ltd 1985

ISBN 0-433-24721-5

Printed in Great Britain by
Biddles Ltd, Guildford, Surrey

(3·6·97)

WA 1141531 2

£.95

70

93

7

3

64

Handbook on Alcoholism
for Health Professionals

Contents

Editor's Foreword

In 1981 on a visit to New Zealand to discuss alcohol problems, I had the pleasure of meeting Dr Ludwig Bieder, one of the authors of this book. Later, he sent me a copy of the *Handbook on Alcoholism for General Practitioners* and I was much impressed by its simple presentation of the basic facts about alcoholism. When Heinemann decided to publish the book in this country I readily agreed to edit it for British readers. This has required two modifications: removal of references to New Zealand practices, and more importantly, a personal decision to modify the emphasis on medical practice.

Alcoholism is a problem which confronts many other health workers besides doctors, and I hope that this useful handbook in its present form will reach a wider audience among the many people who are concerned with the detection and prevention of an increasingly common social problem.

Alex Paton

Preface

After years of comparative indifference, health workers are becoming actively interested in the subject of alcoholism and in the ever increasing number of people presenting with alcohol-related problems. There is now a realisation that, no matter what the specialty or type of practice, everyone needs to be constantly aware of the influence of alcohol on health and sickness.

Unfamiliarity and uncertainty, owing to lack of formal education, make it difficult for some therapists to manage the alcohol-impaired effectively. Sometimes, prejudiced attitudes add to this difficulty.

The Executive Committee of the recently formed New Zealand Medical Society on Alcohol and Alcoholism, recognising these difficulties, encouraged the authors to write this handbook and make it available to all practising health workers.

The handbook is designed to be a practical, ready reference 'bench book' suitable for the busy practitioner, and it is hoped that the brief 'lecture note' format will aid rapid reading and reference.

This is not a treatise on alcoholism, a topic which is still poorly understood and has many areas of controversy. In the interests of brevity and clarity, it has been necessary to take a dogmatic approach on many uncertain and debatable issues which would be given more considered treatment in a standard textbook.

The authors wish to thank the Alcoholic Liquor Advisory Council of New Zealand for encouragement and financial assistance in the preparation and distribution of this publication.

Finally, we would like to dedicate this handbook to Sir Charles Burns who has done so much to transform professional attitudes and behaviour towards alcoholism.

Ludwig Bieder, John O'Hagan, Edwin Whiteside

Introduction

The purpose of this handbook is to assist in making an early diagnosis and effectively managing people with acute or chronic alcohol-related problems.

General Problems

At least 15% of patients admitted to general hospitals have an alcohol-related illness or disability, and in a further 10–20% this is a significant contributing factor to admission.

About 50% of fatal traffic accidents involve alcohol.

A person with a serious alcohol problem usually affects the lives of four others.

Alcohol misuse is now one of the commoner causes of sickness and death.

Too often alcohol is not suspected as the cause until illness is at a late stage, when severe organic impairment is present or when there is a marked alcohol dependence with severe disruption of social function, and treatment is very difficult.

Health workers have a responsibility to become concerned, informed and alert regarding alcohol-related problems, and to be involved in early identification and intervention. An appreciation of the various problems that can occur includes a knowledge of acute disabilities, chronic disabilities, development of the alcohol dependence syndrome, and objective signs of diagnosis of heavy alcohol intake.

Definitions

Introduction

The definitions of alcoholism are numerous, imprecise and controversial. The ones given below are practical. The term 'alcoholism' was originally used to describe the whole range of alcohol-related problems. This can be confusing.

The pronoun 'he' is used throughout the text for the sake of simplicity. As mentioned in the section 'Women and Alcohol', alcoholism is an increasing problem among females.

Alcoholism: any physical, mental or social problem caused by alcohol.
Acute: alcohol intoxication.
Chronic: hazardous drinking,
problem drinking,
alcohol dependence syndrome (classical alcoholism).

These categories grade into one another and many alcoholics may be in a 'grey area'.

The Alcohol Content of Common Drinks

Beer   Tablewine   Sherry   Spirits

	Beer	Tablewine	Sherry	Spirits
10 grams (g) of absolute alcohol (which is equivalent to 1 standard unit) =	½ pint (300 ml)	4 oz (120 ml)	2 oz (60 ml)	1 oz (30 ml)
Grams of absolute alcohol in 100 ml =	2–8	8	16	32
Grams of absolute alcohol per bottle ('standard' bottle size given in parenthesis) =	10–40 (400 ml)	80 (1 litre)	120 (700 ml)	240 (750 ml)
80 grams of absolute alcohol =	4 pints	1 bottle	⅔ bottle	⅓ bottle

* All figures are approximate

Acute Alcoholic Intoxication

Level of intoxication relates to:

1. Blood Alcohol Level (BAL)
   (1 mmol/litre = 4.6 mg/100 ml)

   0–11 mmol/litre (0– 50 mg/100 ml) *usually safe.*
   11–22 mmol/litre (50–100 mg/100 ml) *hazardous if driving.*
   22–44 mmol/litre (100–200 mg/100 ml) *serious intoxication.*
   44–88 mmol/litre (200–400 mg/100 ml) *dangerous intoxication*
   — increased tolerance
   suggests alcohol
   dependency.
   >88 mmol/litre   (>400 mg/100 ml) *potentially lethal.*

2. Other factors such as:

Age and sex.
Tolerance.
Psychological state – fatigue – anxiety.
Expectation of intoxicating effect.
Use of other psychotropic drugs.
General health and nutrition.

The level of BAL varies with:

1. Dose, rate of consumption and concentration of alcohol used.
2. Whether taken on an empty stomach or with meals.
3. Body weight and fat distribution, sex and age.
4. Intake of carbonated drinks which increase the rate of absorption.
5. Variation in rate of alcohol metabolism – may be up to twice as fast in heavy drinkers.

For a 70 kg male a standard drink of 10 g of alcohol will raise the BAL to about 15 mg/100 ml (3 mmol/litre) and will take about 60 minutes to metabolise.

Hazardous Drinking

Characterised by prolonged, regular excessive consumption with a high risk of physical, mental and social complications, but no dependency features.

Prolonged: for about five years or more.
Regular: almost daily (or on a less frequent, regular heavier basis, e.g. Thursday through to Sunday).
Excessive: 60–80 g/day for males,
30–40 g/day for females – predisposition to cirrhosis.
New information suggests these limits may be too high.

No evidence of dependency features except some increased tolerance.
Occasional amnesic 'blackouts'.
May or may not be associated with acute intoxication.
Physical, mental and social complications may or may not be present. If absent, there is a significant risk of developing them in the future.

Look for:
Episodic heavy social drinking to intoxication (memory blackout).
Regular hazardous intake over 60 g ethanol/day.
Increasing psycho-social problems (at home or work).
Acute health problems (accidents or inflammation of stomach, liver, pancreas).

A Treatment Goal of Moderation

Moderation is indicated, at least in the first instance. However, abstinence should be recommended if moderation fails or there is a strong medical contraindication to alcohol.

Moderation may be prompted by the following:

A less regular pattern, e.g. drink-free days.
No more than 30–40 g in any day (three or four standard drinks). Get patient to agree to drinking limits.
Education about alcohol and alcoholism.
Exploring the cues which promote or suppress drinking behaviour.
Tackling precipitating psycho-social problems, e.g. marital or work stress.

Hazardous drinkers may spontaneously return to moderation, e.g. after illness, following a life crisis, with marriage or maturation.

Problem Drinking

Characterised by problems related to alcohol use without dependency or excessive, prolonged regular consumption.

Isolated Acute Intoxication

Accidents.
Crime – violence.
Social misdemeanours.
Acute alcohol induced disease, gastrointestinal haemorrhage, arrhythmia.
Death from acute intoxication.

Continued Drinking with a Medical Contraindication
Peptic ulceration.
Severe obesity.
Unstable insulin-dependent diabetes.
Severe treated hypertension.
Concurrent use of psychotropic drugs.
Other drug interactions.

Miscellaneous Problems

Marital stress.
Poor work performance.

Problem drinking responds usually to simple counselling with family, employer and peer group support.

Alcohol Dependence Syndrome (Classical Alcoholism)

This is characterised by a number of features.

Dependency Features

Increased tolerance.
Narrowing of the drinking pattern – stereotyped drinking.
Amnesic 'blackouts' – memory lapses following acute intoxication.
Withdrawal symptoms – sweats, tremor, nausea, irritability.
Awareness of loss of control (compulsion).
Failed attempts at abstinence.
Preoccupation with drinking.
Drinking to relieve withdrawal symptoms.

High Daily Alcohol Intake

Usually $> 120 \, g/day$.
May decline with end-stage liver and brain damage.
Due to tolerance, intoxication may not be obvious.

Familial Occurrence

Genetic as well as environmental factors.

Wide Range of Organ Damage, Mental and Social Ill-Health

Obscure aetiology, probably multi-factorial.
Ill-health not invariably present in the early stages, not essential to the diagnosis.
Usually a progression of prolonged hazardous drinking.
Often developing after a significant 'life-event', e.g. bereavement, retirement.

Made worse by secondary nutritional and psychological factors.

Occasionally develops 'de novo', or from background of social drinking.

Occurrence

In all social groups.

At any age and in both sexes.

Increasing relevance in women and teenagers recently.

With alcohol in any form.

Commonly Associated Psychological Defence Mechanisms

Make management difficult (see page 31).

Requiring Abstinence as the Treatment Goal

Abstinence or return to moderate drinking can on rare occasions occur spontaneously.

Nevertheless, abstinence is always the treatment goal if the alcohol dependence syndrome exists.

Look for:

Compulsive bouts of drinking with increasing frequency.

Stereotyped drinking lifestyle with regular intake well over 60 g ethanol/day.

High tolerance and withdrawal effects.

Chronic social and health problems.

Neurological disability syndrome.

Relationships of Drinking Categories

This is a rough conceptual guide to the drinking categories of people over 15 years of age. Percentages are speculative and take no account of sex, race or social class. It is estimated that 10% of drinkers consume 66% of the alcohol.

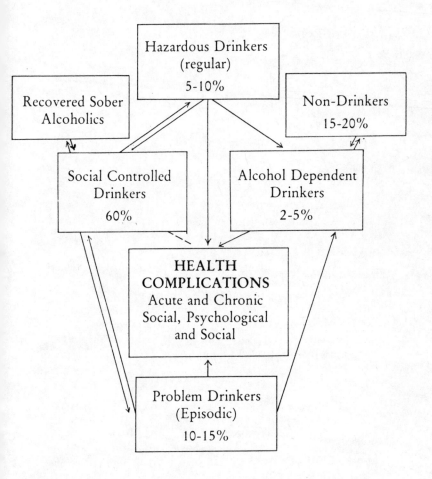

Complications

Physical

These diseases and conditions are not specific or consistently diagnostic of heavy alcohol consumption but should raise suspicion, especially when more than one is present.
Note: Usually appear later than the social and psychological complications.

Key: * = common, E = early (may also be late), L = late.

Cardiovascular

'Holiday Heart' – Cardiac Arrhythmias [*E]
Tachycardia – sinus and paroxysmal.
Ectopic beats.
Atrial fibrillation – chronic and paroxysmal.
After heavy drinking vacation [*E].
May be responsible for higher incidence of sudden death among heavy drinkers.

Cardiomyopathy [L]
With lowered cardiac output and left ventricular failure.
Beriberi heart disease with high output failure and thiamine deficiency.

Hypertension [*E]
May remit partially with abstinence.
Compliance and treatment problems in established hypertension.

Respiratory

Oedema of the Vocal Chords
Hoarseness.

Chronic Bronchitis [*L]
Especially in heavy smokers.

15

Aspiration Pneumonia [L]
Lung abscess.
Empyema.

Bacterial Pneumonia [L]
Poor immune response.
Impaired lung defence mechanisms.

Tuberculosis [L]

Carcinoma of the upper airways

Carcinoma of the Lung [L]

Obstructive sleep apnoea syndrome

Alcohol or Mouth Wash on Breath [*E] *at routine consultation*

'Café Coronary' [E]
Acute laryngeal obstruction by food inhalation (e.g. steak).

Gastrointestinal

Carcinoma [L]
Mouth, pharynx or oesophagus much more common,
especially when combined with smoking.

Furred Unhealthy Tongue [*E]

Dysphagia

Reflux Oesophagitis [*E]
Diminished lower oesophageal sphincter tone.

Haemorrhage [E]
Rupture of oesophageal varices [L].
Mallory-Weiss syndrome [E].

Gastritis (Acute or Chronic) [*E]
Dyspepsia, morning nausea and vomiting.
Gastric erosions and haemorrhage (especially when
combined with aspirin).

Peptic Ulcer [E]

Small intestine
Diarrhoea – chronic or acute [E].
Malabsorption – vitamins,
                amino acids,
                carbohydrates,
                iron?

Liver (four stages) [*E]
1. Abnormal liver function tests (see page 43).
2. Fatty enlargement and tenderness.
3. Alcoholic hepatitis.
4. Cirrhosis-hepatoma [*L].

With portal hypertension, ascites, hepatic coma at an advanced stage.

Pancreas [*E]
Pancreatitis
    Acute, relapsing or chronic.
    Steatorrhoea.
    Pancreatic diabetes.

Haematological

Red cells
Blood loss anaemia – varices and peptic ulcer [E].
Iron deficiency anaemia – nutritional [L].
Megaloblastic anaemia – folate deficiency – nutritional [L].
                                           – malabsorption.
Sideroblastic anaemia – ringed sideroblasts in marrow [L].
Macrocytosis (MCV > 95) [*E]
    Thick macrocytosis
        folate deficiency,
        haemolytic anaemia,
        specifically alcohol-induced.
    Thin macrocytosis
        alcoholic cirrhosis.

Haemolytic anaemia
alcoholic liver disease [L],
stomatocytosis.
Haemochromatosis
may worsen primary familial type [L].
alcoholic cirrhosis occasionally associated with secondary
type.

White cells [E]
Granulocytopenia – with acute infection.
– low grade chronic granulocytopenia.
Impaired lymphocyte/macrophage function.

Platelets [E]
Thrombocytopenia – with acute and chronic intoxication,
– folate deficiency,
– hypersplenism in cirrhosis.

Coagulation [L]
Factor deficiency in alcoholic liver disease.

Neurological

Alcohol should enter into the differential diagnosis of all acute confusional and coma states.

Acute Alcoholic Intoxication [*E]
Confusion, coma and death with respiratory depression, often combined with other drugs.

Hyponatraemic Coma
Beer drinker's water intoxication.

Hyperosmolar Coma
With hypernatraemia in acute intoxication.

Sub-Dural Haematoma [*E]
Accidents common in alcoholics, especially head injury and fractures.

Metabolic Coma
Alcohol-induced hypoglycaemia, keto and lactic acidosis.

Convulsions [L]
Usually grand mal.
Acute intoxication.
Acute withdrawal.
Brain damaged chronic alcoholic.
Alcohol-induced fits in idiopathic epilepsy.

Alcoholic Withdrawal Syndrome (see page 64) [*L]

Wernicke's Encephalopathy [L]
Ophthalmoplegia.
Ataxia – nystagmus.
Mental disturbance – confusion – coma.
Responsive to thiamine.

Korsakoff's Psychosis [*L]
Disorder of recent memory.
Lack of judgement.
Confusion.
Confabulation.
Not usually thiamine responsive.

Alcoholic Dementia [*]
Cerebro-cortical degeneration and atrophy.
More marked in the frontal and pre-frontal cortex.
Probably the commonest form of alcoholic brain damage.
Significance apparent since CAT scanning and sophisticated
    psychometric testing used.
May be more common than alcoholic liver disease.
Subtle changes may be present even in early hazardous
    drinking.
May have implications for treatment success.

Early features: visuo-motor, visuo-spatial skill impairment,
                impaired adaptive abilities and new concept
                    formation,
                impaired self-criticism,
                impaired problem-solving,
                intelligence and verbal skills may remain
                    intact.

Late features: serious intellectual impairment,
marked loss of judgement,
memory impairment.

Cerebellar Degeneration [L]
Ataxia.

Polyneuropathy [*L]
Peripheral sensory-motor neuropathy.
Including autonomic neuropathy.
Peripheral nerve pressure palsies, e.g. radial nerve.
'Saturday-night palsy'.

Unusual and Rare [L]
Central pontine myelinosis.
Marchiafava – Bignami's disease (encephalopathy and
   dementia).
Pellagra (vitamin B deficiency).

(Tobacco) Alcohol Amblyopia [L]
Bilateral optic neuritis with central scotoma.
Nutritional deficiencies.
Vitamin B_{12} effective.

Nutritional

Vitamin Deficiencies [L]
B_1, B_6, folate – most common, but vitamins A, C and B_{12}
also.

Mineral Deficiences [L]
Magnesium, zinc, iron, calcium, phosphate.

Malnutrition [*L]
Protein and calorie – thin.
Protein only – often fat. 'Empty' calorie syndrome.
Low serum albumin and pre-albumin.

Metabolic

Hypoglycaemia – with fasting.

Hyperglycaemia – transient glucose intolerance with or without diabetes.

Ketoacidosis – with fasting and dehydration with or without diabetes.

Lactic acidosis – associated liver disease with or without diabetes.

Hypertriglyceridaemia [*E].

Elevated high density lipoprotein cholesterol [*E].

Hyperuricaemia – provocation of gout [*E].

Attacks of porphyria.

Hyperosmolality – in acute intoxication.

Poor Diabetic Control
With insulin, or oral hypoglycaemics, or reducing diets [*E].

Endocrine

Adrenal
ACTH-mediated, alcohol-induced rise in plasma cortisol [L].

'Pseudo-Cushing's' syndrome in chronic alcoholics.

Primary or secondary, chronic adrenocortical insufficiency.

Alcohol-induced medullary catecholamine hypersecretion.

Possible cause of sweating, tachycardia and hypertension.

Thyroid
In alcoholic cirrhosis, low serum thyroid binding proteins and low T_4 simulate hypothyroidism but thyroid stimulating hormone and free thyroxine index normal. Peripheral conversion of T_4 to T_3 also diminished giving low T_3 levels [L].

Gonadal
Decreased serum testosterone levels – even in absence of liver disease [L].

Direct testicular effect.

Low testosterone and high oestogen levels in alcoholic cirrhosis [L].

Feminisation – gynaecomastia, testicular atrophy, spider naevi.

Loss of libido [*E].

Pituitary
Suppression of antidiuretic hormone with water diuresis [*E].
Inhibition of oxytocin release – use to control premature
  labour.

Skin

Infections [L], *boils*

Unexplained bruising

Paronychia [L]

Clubbing of fingers [L]

Dupuytren's contracture [*L]

Abrasions [*E]

Lacerations [*E]

Hyperpigmentation [*L]

Vascular spiders (naevi) [*L]

Palmar erythema [*L]

Sweating of hands and feet [*E]

Facial

Puffiness [*E]

Vasodilatation and flushing [*E]

Rosacea

Parotid hyperplasia [L]

Conjunctivae [*E]
Vessels engorged.
Corkscrew vessels in sclera.

Musculoskeletal

Muscle [L]
Acute rhabdomyolysis.
Chronic myopathy.
Raised muscle enzymes.

Skeletal [L]
Osteoporosis and aseptic bone necrosis.

Traumatic and Accidental [*E]

Increased tendency to accident – trauma.
Single vehicle accidents.
'Closing time' accidents.
Repeated accidents.
Pedestrian and cycle accidents.
Drinking and driving offences.
Drowning accidents in adults.
Hypothermia.
Accidental falls.
Unexplained falls.
Industrial accidents.
Unexplained burns.
Unexplained house fires.

The Fetal Alcohol Syndrome

Research findings since 1968 have established the fetal alcohol syndrome as a serious clinical entity.

Alcohol crosses the placenta and equilibrates at the same concentration in the maternal and fetal circulation. Studies indicate that the effect on the fetus is related to the dosage, quantity and frequency. The fetus is more vulnerable to the teratogenic effects of alcohol during the period of organogenesis in the first 12 weeks of pregnancy. Later in pregnancy, alcohol produces fetal growth retardation and failure of brain maturation. The fetus may be affected even when the dose, by many people's standards, is not considered socially excessive.

Characteristics of the Fetal Alcohol Syndrome

Not all features need be present or at an advanced degree.

Most Commonly Seen

Growth retardation.
Small-for-dates babies (below 10th percentile in length and weight).
Increased neonatal death rate.
Slow physical development in the first few years of life.

Frequently Seen

Mental deficiency in varying degrees. Sometimes associated with microcephaly.

Less Frequently Seen

Physical malformations.

Head and facial deformities (microcephaly, squint, microphthalmia, short palpebral fissures, ptosis, flattening of maxilla, thin upper lip).
Cardiac defects.
Joint and limb abnormalities.

Spontaneous Abortion

Two recent reports indicate a seriously increased risk of spontaneous abortion – usually second trimester – with heavy and even modest alcohol consumption.

Advice for the Pregnant Woman

Heavy drinking, more than four standard drinks (40 g alcohol/day), places the fetus at serious risk.
Isolated intoxication, *especially in the first trimester*, is likely to be a risk to the fetus.
Less heavy drinking, two to four standard drinks per day, probably increases the risk to the fetus.
More research is needed to confirm the safety of light drinking (one standard drink per day or less).
There is no established safe lower limit for the intake of alcohol during pregnancy.

The prudent course is to abstain from all alcohol during pregnancy.

In giving this advice doctors should try not to promote excessive anxiety in those who continue light drinking, or guilt feelings in those who have borne an abnormal child after taking alcohol in pregnancy.

Drug–Alcohol Interactions

Drug–alcohol interactions are frequently encountered these days because both substances are widely used (Table).

These interactions may take place at any stage during their absorption, their transport in the plasma, distribution in the tissues, at the receptor sites, during metabolism, or during the eventual excretion.

Important Interactions between Alcohol and Drugs

Acute ingestion of alcohol:	*Chronic alcoholism:*
Inhibits drug metabolism.	Decreases metabolism of drugs
Prolongs action of	by liver.
Barbiturates	Delays action of
Opiates	Barbiturates
Antidepressants	Sedatives
Tranquillisers	Diazepam
Diazepam	Anticonvulsants
Antihistamines	Oral hypoglycaemics
Betablockers	Anticoagulants.
Oral hypoglycaemics	
Anticoagulants	
Paracetamol	
Dextropropoxyphene	
(in Distalgesic).	

One is therefore faced with an enormous number of possibilities and some doctors will tend to ignore the problem while a few may over-react.

Ethanol is mainly metabolised in the liver by a variety of enzymes – mainly alcohol dehydrogenase, but also by the microsomal enzymes. Chronic ingestion of alcohol stimulates these enzymes and speeds up the metabolism and the break-down of alcohol and other drugs, whereas acute isolated alcohol intoxication inhibits the enzyme systems and therefore slows down the metabolism of drugs.

The interactions may be antagonistic, synergistic, potentiating or mutually neutralising in their effect.

Sedatives, Tranquillisers, Analgesics

Ethanol is basically a central nervous system depressant and therefore will have an additive effect when given with tranquillisers, sedatives, sleeping drugs and analgesics, whereas amphetamine, caffeine, cocaine and possibly nicotine should have an antagonistic effect when co-administered with alcohol.

Therefore, acute casual alcohol ingestion will prolong the action of barbiturates, whereas in prolonged administration of both drugs, tolerance and more efficient metabolism will result.

Non-barbiturate hypnotics like glutethamide belong psychopharmacologically to the same class as barbiturates and have, by and large, the same synergistic effect when taken with alcohol.

Trichlorethanol

A combination of *chloralhydrate* and alcohol constitutes the well-known 'Mickey Finn' or 'Knockout Drops': trichlorethanol acts by inhibition of acetaldehyde dehydrogenase and also has a synergistic action on the conversion of ethanol to acetaldehyde.

All tranquillisers are central nervous system (CNS) depressants and are additive in their ability to impair psychomotor function and cause CNS depression when given with alcohol.

The *phenothiazines* and *haloperidol* additionally are prone to produce hypotension, and *meprobamate* produces synergistic depression, whereas the *benzodiazepines* have little or no additive effect when taken with alcohol.

The *tricyclic antidepressants* are said to have an increased risk of causing paralytic ileus and CNS depressant effects when given with alcohol.

Monoamine oxidase inhibitors (MAO) inhibit liver and other enzyme systems and thereby increase the depressant effect of alcohol, and may also cause tyramine-containing alcohols like some wines (Chianti, red wines and sherries) to exert a hypertensive effect when taken with MAO inhibitors.

Antihistamines potentiate the CNS depression produced by alcohol and are therefore particularly contraindicated for drivers.

Narcotics including dextropropoxyphene depress the CNS and have, in this respect, a synergistic action with alcohol.

Reserpine also has a synergistic action but no direct effect on the rate of alcohol metabolism.

Analgesics

Generally should not be given with alcohol – *aspirin* and *salicylates* in particular interfere with platelet aggregation, and chronic alcohol use (due to the effect on the bone marrow activity) could potentiate this effect on the platelets and produce a state of hypocoagulability and, with it, a tendency to haemorrhage.

Anticoagulants

The interaction between alcohol and the *warfarin* type anticoagulants is not well-defined – but even minor liver damage by alcohol may diminish the formation of prothrombin and, with it, an enhanced response to anticoagulants. Stimulation of the microsomal enzymes may, however, have the opposite effect.

Anticonvulsants

Phenytoin especially is metabolised at a faster rate by persons who drink alcohol. Excessive drinking may therefore result in seizures in a person previously well-controlled on anti-convulsants. This is due to microsomal enzyme induction by alcohol.

Antihypertensives

Ethanol has been shown to produce an additive hypotensive effect, presumably due to renal and peripheral vasodilatation.

Ethanol also lowers the blood sugar due to impairment of gluconeogenesis. The hypoglycaemic activity of insulin may also be increased – this mainly being a problem in those with depleted hepatic glycogen stores.

Betablockers

Decrease liver blood flow and therefore lower the metabolism of most drugs as well as of alcohol. Elevated blood alcohol levels remain longer.

Stimulants

Amphetamine, caffeine, methylphenidate, antagonise the effect of alcohol to some degree but may produce tachycardia and raise the blood pressure and add these to the effects of acute alcohol intoxication.

Nicotine

Probably the most commonly-used stimulant and is particularly abused by alcoholics who are almost invariably heavy smokers.

Pharmacologically nicotine has a caffeine-like effect and therefore antagonises the effect of alcohol.

Psychologically probably the opposite effect.

Disulfiram-like Reaction (see page 74)

Ethacrynic acid, phenylbutazone, and probably *metronidazole* inhibit liver alcohol dehydrogenase and therefore may keep the ethanol blood level higher and more prolonged. Metronidazole may produce a disulfiram-like reaction if taken with alcohol.

Antibiotics such as *griseofulvin, sulphonamides, chloramphenicol* and *nitrofurantoin* may provoke a mild disulfiram-like reaction when given with alcoholic drinks.

Hypoglycaemic agents such as *acetohexamide, chlorpropamide, tolbutamide* also have a mild disulfiram-like action with the addition of alcohol.

General Anaesthetics

Increased tolerance to alcohol usually increases requirements for general anaesthetics. Acute intoxication lowers the requirements.

Naloxone

This morphine antagonist possibly counteracts alcoholic intoxication.

Psychological

General

There is no one alcoholic personality. The pre-morbid personality and mental health of alcoholics is probably no different from the general population. Most, but not all, psychological problems in alcoholics are secondary to the effects of drinking. In some, the psychiatric disorder (e.g. affective disorder, psychopathic personality) is primary and precedes the abnormal drinking behaviour.

There are almost no psychological symptoms or syndromes which cannot be caused or exacerbated by alcohol, and other drug misuse. These must be considered in every psychological presentation. The diagnostic possibilities cover the whole field of psychiatry and only the most common manifestations can be listed in the space available in this handbook.

Common Psychological Presentations

Suicide attempts and suicide.
Depression.
Anxiety.
Phobic states.
Fugue states.
Hyperexcitability and rage states.
Morbid jealousy, the 'Othello' syndrome.
Paranoid reactions.
Schizoid reactions.
Insomnia.
Psychopathic and sociopathic behaviour.
Cognitive and memory defects (see page 18).

Consider alcoholism every time a tranquilliser, antidepressant or hypnotic is prescribed.

Sexual Problems

Loss of libido.
Hypogonadism.
Secondary impotence and premature ejaculation, ejaculatory incompetence.
Forcing sexual relations on partner.
Sexual deviancy, e.g. incest, sexual molestation of children, rape.

Social

These are the earliest and most frequent complications of alcohol misuse. The complete range of social disorders can be produced by, or associated with, alcohol misuse.

General

Isolation from family and community activities.
Life revolving around drinking activities.
Increased frequency of driving accidents.
Increase in acts of violence and crime.
Financial problems.
Legal problems.

At Work

Frequent absenteeism, especially Monday and Friday and after pay day.
Frequent and varied medical excuses for absence from work.
Impaired job performance, promotion failure.
Threat of job loss and history of gaps in work, frequent changes of employment.
Industrial accidents.
Early retirement.

Common Effects of Excessive Alcohol Consumption within the Family

The Alcoholic

Denies the alcohol problem, blames others, forgets and tells stories for self-defence and protection against humiliation, attack and criticism from others in the family.

Spends money required for day-to-day family needs on alcohol.

Ignores bills, debts pile up.

Becomes unpredictable and impulsive in behaviour.

Resorts to verbal and physical abuse in place of honest, open talk.

Loses trust of family, relatives and friends.

Experiences increased sexual arousal but reduced function.

Has unpredictable mood swings, 'Jekyll and Hyde' personality.

Uses devious and manipulative behaviour to divert attention from drinking problem.

The Spouse/Partner

Often tries to hide and deny the existing problem of the alcoholic partner.

Takes on the responsibilities of the other person, carrying the load of two and perpetuating the spouse/partner dependence.

Takes a job to get away from the problem, and/or to maintain financial security.

Finds it difficult to be open and honest because of resentment, anger, hurt feelings and shame.

Avoids sexual contact, and may seek separation or divorce.

May over-protect the children, neglect them, and/or use them for emotional support.

Shows gradual social withdrawal and isolation.

May lose feelings of self-respect and self-worth.

May use alcohol or prescription drugs in an effort to cope.

May present to the doctor with anxiety, depression or psychosomatic symptoms.

The Children

Are at increased risk to develop alcohol dependency themselves.

May be victims of birth defects (from maternal alcohol use).

May be torn between two parents; in being loyal to one, they rouse the anger of the other.

May be deprived of emotional and physical support, and lack trust in anyone.

Avoid peer group activities, especially in the home, out of fear and shame.

Learn destructive and negative ways of dealing with problems and getting attention.

May lose sight of values, standards, and goals because of the absence of consistent, strong parenting. Petty crime, school failure, etc.

Suffer a diminishing sense of self-worth as a significant member of the family.

Diagnosis and Assessment

Problems in Diagnosis and Management

Early detection leads to more successful intervention.

Problems of Definition

Controversial – scores of definitions.
Those used in this handbook are practical.
Concept is widening to include earlier non-dependent problems.

Is it a Disease? – 'Sickness or Sin'

Regardless of the semantic debate it is convenient and practical to regard it as a disease, at least in the dependent phase.
Morbidity and mortality demand concern and intervention.

Early Diagnosis can be Difficult

Can present as any physical, psychological, or social pathology.
The great mimic of modern medicine.
Often concealed or denied by patient, spouse, employer and doctor.

Negative Attitudes of Health Professionals

Major barrier to effectiveness – needs understanding.
Reflect community attitudes and poor professional training.
Ambivalence as to whether it is a self-inflicted, bad habit, needing a moralistic, punitive approach or a misfortune, needing a non-judgemental, caring approach.
Personal drinking behaviour and experiences influence attitudes.

Anti-social alcoholic behaviour is offensive. This makes it difficult to develop positive and caring responses.

Compare attitudes to other illness (lung cancer) which may be 'self-inflicted', or sickness associated with bizarre behaviour (frontal lobe tumour).

Difficulties with the Denial Response and Manipulative Behaviour in Alcoholism

Health workers expect co-operation and honesty.

Denial, dishonesty and manipulation encourage the view 'that alcoholics can't be helped, until they ask for it'.

These defence mechanisms need to be seen as an intrinsic part of the disease (see next section).

We should learn strategies to combat these defences.

Approach to the Alcoholic: Some General Principles

Everyone has his own personal style. Remember the doctor is in a most powerful position, especially if there is evidence of physical complications.

General

Alcoholics have low self-esteem. The health worker needs to convince them of his care and concern by devoting time and interest.

He needs to remain 'non-judgemental', separating distaste for the 'disease' and its consequences from concern for the client.

The approach should be firm and realistic. Based on fact. Empathetic rather than sympathetic.

While heavy coercion may be needed, conflict for its own sake should be avoided. The individual may not return. He finally makes his own decision.

Establish empathy. Build up the usually shattered personality.

Time

Many people claim they do not have enough time to manage the alcoholic.

Remember

It can be as destructive as cancer or heart disease and deserves the same level of attention.

If you do not have the time or interest, you have a duty to seek help or refer on to an assessment centre, treatment facility or specialist colleague.

The family/personal doctor has a great advantage and can often complete diagnosis and assessment in three 20–30 minute consultations.

If you ignore the 'alcoholic' you will spend much more fruitless time over the years treating secondary complications in him and his family.

The recovered alcoholic and his family will be among your most grateful customers.

Laboratory Tests in the Assessment of Alcoholism

Early diagnosis is often difficult in the face of strong denials which are frequently encountered.

Laboratory tests can, however, provide objective evidence of heavy drinking in almost every case. These tests can also monitor compliance, further progress, and detect liver cell damage, as well as non-hepatic complications.

MCV (Mean Cell Volume) of erythrocytes is elevated at 95 or above in well over 60% of cases with heavy alcohol intake, especially women. This may or may not be associated with folate deficiency or alcoholic liver disease.

GGT (Gamma Glutamyl Transpeptidase) is an enzyme originating mainly in the liver and is increased in hepatoma, hepatic secondaries, in cholestasis, and can be increased by drugs inducing microsomal enzymes (barbiturates, phenytoin). It can, however, also be increased by continued heavy alcohol intake in up to 75% of cases examined, even in the absence of major alcoholic liver disease. The test is cheap and simple to carry out. Five days of total abstinence will produce a marked fall or return to normal, unless there is hepatocellular damage, pancreatic, renal or intestinal disease. Isolated acute intoxication does not usually cause a rise in this enzyme.

ALT (Alanine Transaminase; SGPT Serum Glutamic Pyruvic Transaminase) is mainly used to monitor progress. If elevated in heavy drinkers it will go down by 50% in about three weeks' time and should return to normal after about 4–6 weeks' abstinence unless the patient has chronic hepatocellular damage.

ALP (Alkaline Phosphatase) is often elevated in alcoholic liver disease but is not specific for alcohol or liver disease.

Breathalyser Tests can at times be very helpful in the

diagnosis of heavy and possibly regular alcohol intake. They should therefore be used in accident and emergency departments and possibly in all other outpatient clinics, as well as in doctors' consulting rooms. They should be part of biochemical screening of all acute adult admissions to hospital.

Alcohol Breath Level

100 mg/100 ml (22 mmol/litre) at a routine consultation.
150 mg/100 ml (33 mmol/litre) without signs of intoxication.
300 mg/100 ml (66 mmol/litre) at any time.

All suggest tolerance indicating alcohol dependence or very heavy, hazardous consumption. (The results of *Blood Alcohol Spot Checks* have the same significance.)

Assessment Strategies

Take Your Time

A chronic condition – no hurry unless a crisis.
But this time may be your only chance – make the most of
   it.

Underplay the Subject at Early Contacts

Defences may be raised and client may not return.
Avoid the emotive word 'alcoholic' at early contacts.
'Alcohol problem' is a less threatening alternative.
Delay taking a detailed drinking history until confidence is
   gained.

Get to Know the Client and Gain His Confidence

Interview. A good medical, social and 'life events' history.
Family history of alcoholism.
Physical examination and investigation.
Laboratory tests (e.g. MCV, GGT).
Interview spouse, family and employer. (There are problems
   of confidentiality with this. Permission required, especially
   for employer.)
Alcoholism questionnaire (e.g. MAST, CAGE) answered by
   patient, spouse, or family (see Appendix 1).
Remember the spouse may also have an alcohol problem.
Even if they have no alcohol problem, the spouse and family
   members often strongly deny the individual has one, and
   can be just as disturbed as the alcoholic.
Be aware of the 'high-risk' occupations.

Take a Detailed Drinking History from Client and/or Spouse

This must be detailed as people often minimise and deny.

Avoid hostility. Try not to suggest that intake is abnormally high. On the contrary, expression of surprise at its low level sometimes encourages a more realistic response.

Establish the alcohol intake, its timing and location, on an average day or week.

Convert this into grams of pure alcohol daily (see Table on page 4).

Enquire about the weekly expenditure on alcohol.

Always enquire about other drug usage, e.g. prescribed, over-the-counter, or illicit. Poly-drug abuse is very common.

Enquire about frequency and circumstances of intoxication.

Enquire about the drinking pattern and its development over the years.

Look for other signs of addictive behaviour, e.g. smoking, obesity.

Find Out about Dependence Symptoms

Increased tolerance – gulping drinks to get a rapid 'high'.

Narrowing of the drinking pattern, stereotyped drinking.

Amnesic 'blackouts' – memory lapses following acute intoxication.

Withdrawal symptoms – sweats, tremor, nausea, irritability.

Awareness of loss of control.

Failed attempts at abstinence.

Preoccupation with drinking.

Drinking to relieve withdrawal symptoms, e.g. first thing in morning.

Try to Classify the Alcohol Problem

No problem.
Isolated problem drinking.

Early hazardous drinking.
Advanced hazardous drinking.
Early alcohol dependence.
Advanced alcohol dependence.

List the Problems Caused by Alcohol in Each Specific Area of Life

Marital	Legal/Criminal
Family	Physical
Social	Emotional/Psychiatric
Occupational	Spiritual
Financial	

Finally Confront the Individual

With each specific problem and harmful effect alcohol is having on his or her life.

If Diagnosis Still in Doubt

Refer to alcoholism specialist for opinion – if subject agreeable.
Suggest abstinence or moderate drinking and review with spouse in 3–6 weeks.

Check List – Physical Examination

General Appearance

Tremor, sweating, irritability, slurred speech, alcoholic facies, conjunctival engorgement, puffy eyes, poor nutrition, unkempt appearance.

Mouth

Coated, inflamed or atrophic tongue, periodontal disease, alcohol or mouthwash on the breath.

Liver

Jaundice, hepatic enlargement and tenderness, splenomegaly, signs of portal hypertension.

Stigmata of liver disease: palmar erythema, parotid swelling, spider naevi, clubbing, gynaecomastia, testicular atrophy.

Skin

Burns, bruises, injuries.
Dupuytren's contracture.

Neuromuscular

Confusion, intoxication, hallucinations, poor recent memory, ataxia, peripheral neuritis, muscle wasting and tenderness.

Blood Tests

Routine	Specific

Red Cell Count
   MCV must be included
	If anaemia, liver pathology or
	acute infection:
	   White Cell and Platelet Counts
	   ESR
	If myopathy suspected:
	   Creatine Phosphokinase

Liver Function Tests
   Must include GGT, ALP, ALT
	If liver pathology suspected:
	   Prothrombin Time

Blood Alcohol Level	If abdominal symptoms: Amylase

Lipids (Fasting)
   (Alcohol interferes with
   metabolism of fat)
	If anaemia, macrocytosis or poor
	nutrition present:
	   Folate

Uric Acid
   (Alcohol may cause gout in
   susceptible people)
	If poor nutrition, neuropathy,
	cardiomyopathy or CNS changes:
	   Transketolase (Thiamine Assay)
	If acutely ill:
	   Urea, Electrolytes, Magnesium,
	   Calcium, Glucose, pH,
	   Osmolality
	If liver pathology confirmed or
	illicit drug use suspected:
	   Hepatitis B Surface Antigen

Flow Chart for Diagnosis and Management

	Psycho-Social Problems	Drinking Behaviour & Consumption	Medical Problems
Early High Index of Suspicion			
Seek Specific Confirmation	Interviews with Relatives and Friends or Employer	Drinking History & Questionnaire e.g. (MAST)	Full Examination & Laboratory Tests (liver biopsy), etc.

Specific Diagnosis and Management Plan

	Alcohol-Related Disability 'Hazardous or Problem Drinking'	Alcohol Dependence Syndrome 'Compulsive or Addictive Drinking'
Average Ethanol Intake		
Diagnostic Classification		
Management Plan	Monthly Review of Progress in Reducing or Avoiding Alcohol related problems	Referral for Inpatient Medical Care (e.g. withdrawal and counselling for alcohol abstinence)

Note: The prescribing of another chemical that may produce dependence (e.g. minor tranquilliser) is no substitute for a proper diagnostic or management plan.

The Alcoholic's Defence Mechanisms

General

A common and integral part of the alcohol dependence syndrome.

Often subconscious and not essentially wilful.

Psychological coping responses to the situation where drinking is harmful and yet cannot be controlled.

Influenced by guilt and low self-esteem.

Must be recognised and understood for successful intervention.

Sometimes they can be exploited by a therapist in the early phases of rehabilitation.

Too often the therapist 'gives up', interpreting these responses as dishonesty or deviousness and assuming the patient cannot be helped until he wants to be.

The Defence Mechanisms

Denial: Inability to recognise the problem – very common.

Minimising: Making the problem appear much less serious than it is.

Rationalisation: Making apparently reasonable excuses to justify behaviour.

Projection: Placing responsibility for behaviour on another person or situation.

Intellectualisation: Recognising the problem but with detachment and lack of conviction.

Diversion: Changing the subject to avoid discussion of the problem.

Hostility: Becoming angry and aggressive to avoid discussion of the problem.

Confrontation Techniques

General

Very valuable in combating denial and bringing the more advanced, dependent alcoholic to treatment.

Requires skill, experience and a firm, non-judgemental, concerned approach.

It creates a crisis for the alcoholic instead of waiting for the dangerous crises of the 'rock-bottom' state.

Methods

The individual needs to be sober and preferably through acute withdrawal.

Confrontation is led by the therapist, preferably along with the spouse and, if indicated, older children, employer, close friend (non-alcoholic), recovered alcoholic, clergyman.

The strategy of confrontation and treatment options should be well-prepared beforehand with those involved, and they should be convinced of its necessity and propriety.

Care, concern and desire to help the victim are the basis of all action.

The subject is honestly and firmly confronted with all the harm he and his loved ones are suffering as a result of his drinking. Specific incidents of harmful behaviour are highlighted.

Emphasis is placed on the dangers to health, quality of life, and the risks of early death if drinking continues.

The subject usually produces the common defence mechanisms. These need to be recognised and countered, using the authority and experience of the therapist if necessary.

Emphasis should be laid on the damaging effect of alcohol and the need to take treatment rather than on a search for the causes of the problem.

At this stage avoid deep involvement in the often complex psychological and social problems. They are unlikely to be resolved while the brain is still suffering from acute or chronic alcohol impairment.

Self-esteem is enhanced by pointing out the victim's good qualities and the excellent prospects, if alcohol can be avoided.

An immediate and realistic treatment plan is given and every help offered to achieve its success.

Heavy Coercion

It has more risks but may be necessary if the alcoholic is in dire straits, has entrenched denial or brain damage.

Close, immediate, follow-up support is essential.

Threats should be made reluctantly, emphasising the concern to help the alcoholic to a happier life, but with a stated, firm conviction that they will be carried out if necessary.

Coercion may take the form of:

> *Threat* of a spouse to leave the home.
> Loss of employment.
> Loss of driver's licence.
> Jail sentence.
> Loss of professional licence to practise.
> Compulsory admission and treatment.

Concluding Contract

Whatever the outcome, try and make a contract with the alcoholic emphasising your continuing concern for him and asking for his co-operation in the future.

1. If treatment is accepted, that he will:
      Give it an adequate trial.
      Consult you before opting out of therapy.

2. If treatment is not accepted but he wishes to try and abstain or control drinking by himself, that he will:
   Return to you regularly with his spouse for follow-up.
   Accept treatment if his own efforts fail.
3. If all help is rejected, that he will contact you again if at any time in the future help is needed.

Never give up hope. Confront the dependent alcoholic sincerely and caringly at every contact. Your efforts will often bear fruit some time in the future.

Treatment Referral

There are many treatment approaches. It is necessary to match the treatment programme with the needs of the individual. In making these decisions, the following should be taken into account:

The range of facilities available in your area.
Age – special consideration given to the young and very old.
Degree of denial, insight, motivation and co-operation.
Amount of social support – spouse, family, friends, employer, community.
Physical complications – may need initial general hospital or outpatient management.
Degree of brain damage – psychometric testing may be necessary.
Individual preference, e.g. AA, counselling or behavioural approach.
Counselling skill, knowledge of alcoholism and time available to the therapist.
Level of alcohol problem.
The availability of an effective employee assistance programme at the individual's work place.

Dependent Alcoholics

Abstinence should always be the goal.
Early – with low denial, good physical health and good social support:
AA, outpatient counselling alone or in combination.
More advanced – with significant denial, dubious co-operation, poor social support or ill health:
Inpatient programme with follow-up AA and/or outpatient counselling.

Late stage brain-damaged:
> As for more advanced cases. If repeated relapse, consider sheltered accommodation or long-term residential care.

Hazardous Drinkers

Moderation and controlled drinking can be an initial option for non-dependent drinkers.

Mature hazardous drinker with good insight may only need simple education, encouragement and follow-up by therapist.

Young immature hazardous drinker with insight may respond to controlled drinking programme of behavioural type.

More advanced hazardous drinker with poor insight and some denial will need longer outpatient counselling from an alcoholism service with an initial goal of moderation and an option of abstinence if this fails.

The Job is not Finished After Initial Assessment or Referral

The therapist:

Must continue to support and counsel the alcoholic, spouse and family.

Should introduce the spouse and family to support agencies such as Al-Anon and Alateen.

Prognosis in the Alcohol Dependence Syndrome

There are many variables and uncertainties. Pessimistic predictions are, on occasion, surprisingly wrong.

In assessing the prognosis, the following points are significant:

Age, severity and length of dependence, social class.
Response to previous therapy.
Degree of denial and insight.
The presence of irreversible physical complications, ill-health, or psychiatric disorder.
The presence of significant brain damage.
The continued support of spouse, family and community.
Stable employment with supportive employer.
The availability of appropriate and successful treatment programmes.
Willingness to attend AA or other support groups.

Outcome of Treatment in the Alcohol Dependence Syndrome

Scientific evidence is difficult to interpret because of many variables:

The wide range of therapies offered in varied situations.
The selection of patients with a wide variety of prognostic characteristics.
Variable definitions of success, for example,

Lifelong abstinence,
Lifelong abstinence with relapses,
Temporary abstinence,
Improved drinking pattern,
Improved personal, family and occupational function while abnormal drinking continues.

Given these difficulties of interpretation, success rates of between 20–80% are quoted. Successful outcome is frequent enough to include alcohol dependence among the most favourable of the chronic disorders encountered in medical practice.

Untreated, long-term spontaneous recovery is rare and the condition is often progressive and sometimes fatal.

The 'Absent' Alcoholic

When the 'Real' Victim is Absent

Alcoholism is a 'family disease'.

Often the non-alcoholic spouse or children will present social or emotional problems (see page 34). They may be just as sick as the dependent alcoholic.

It is essential to try and engage the alcoholic personally.

When the alcoholic cannot be engaged or will not accept help, the therapist must continue to support, counsel and educate the family members.

They frequently respond to the stress and trauma in a negative, destructive way, compounding family problems, and enabling the alcoholic to continue drinking (co-alcoholism).

Ignorance, bewilderment and embarrassment lead on to guilt, bitterness and hostility.

Even if the alcoholic stops drinking, recovery is incomplete (the dry drunk) until personal, marital and family psychopathology has been resolved in family or marriage counselling.

When the Non-alcoholic Spouse or Child is Ambivalent or Denies the Problem, Gain their Confidence by:

Not moving too quickly.

Showing concern and willingness to help.

Always remaining non-judgemental and empathetic.

Confirming that you understand their difficulties, frustrations, and have known and helped others with similar problems.

Congratulating them for their courage and wisdom in coming forward for help.

Working with the Non-alcoholic Spouse and Children

Educate them about the condition of alcoholism and alcoholic behaviour.

Try to remove their *guilt* feeling that they may have caused the problem.

Point out those negative responses which *enable* the spouse to continue drinking.

Encourage *detachment* from the problem – the alcoholic finally has to make his own decision.

Discourage *covering-up* for the alcoholic.

At a sober time encourage honest *confrontation* without anger or reproach.

Encourage *openness* and candour about the situation with the alcoholic and his friends.

Try and *divert energies* away from attempts to alter the alcoholic's lifestyle. Concentrate on a constructive evaluation of the spouse's own emotional responses and behaviour.

Encourage them to get additional continuing support by joining *Al-Anon* or *Alateen* and, if necessary, refer for more intensive individual or family counselling.

If marriage break-up seems inevitable the therapist should try and guide them towards a *constructive separation*, and successful assumption of their new roles.

Engaging the 'Absent' Alcoholic

It is essential to engage the alcoholic personally. This is often difficult and sometimes a degree of subterfuge is necessary.

Some possibilities are:

To wait until he comes for consultation or advice. This is unreliable and may cause dangerous delay.

When the alcoholic visits the therapist, it may be unwise to quickly focus on his own problem. Time is needed to gain his confidence and make an unbiased appraisal of the diagnosis and the family dynamics.

Return visits may be ensured by getting an agreement to some joint counselling interviews when the focus can gradually be shifted to the basic alcoholic problem.

On occasions a return visit can be secured by the necessity for a blood pressure check or the follow-up of laboratory tests.

Management and
Rehabilitation

Common Deficiencies in Management

Ignoring the diagnosis except for the obvious end-stage or 'skid row' stereotype, e.g. in upper and professional social classes, women, adolescents.

Treating the complication (e.g. peptic ulceration, or insomnia) and ignoring the basic problem – alcoholism.

Late diagnosis leading to treatment failure and relapse. This encourages the erroneous belief that treatment is ineffective (cf. late diagnosis of cancer).

Failure to appreciate that it is often a chronic relapsing disorder. Rejecting the alcoholic after a relapse (cf. asthma, or rheumatoid arthritis). A drinking lapse on the contrary should prompt the therapist to make an immediate concerned intervention.

Note: Treating only withdrawal symptoms and medical complications without long-term rehabilitation, serves only to enable the alcoholic to become well enough to return to his previous drinking pattern and cycle of destruction. All available means must be used to bring him to long-term treatment and rehabilitation.

Alcohol Withdrawal Syndrome

Occurs:

In very heavy and dependent drinkers 6 to 48 hours after cessation of drinking as the result of a sudden lowering of the blood alcohol level.

Possibly because of rebound hypersensitivity of neuro-receptors producing hyperexcitability of the brain and autonomic nervous system.

Important because it:

May be the first hint of an alcohol problem.

Provides an opportunity for intervention in the known alcoholic.

Enters into the differential diagnosis of many acute disease states.

May be lethal if associated with
    an intercurrent illness, accident or operation,
    underlying alcohol-induced disease, e.g. cirrhosis, pancreatitis,
    malnutrition and general ill-health or delirium tremens.

Description

Early Mild Phase

Alcohol may still be on the breath and at low levels in the blood.

Tremor.

Sweats, flushing.

Anxiety, agitation.

Insomnia, restlessness.

Nausea, vomiting.

Alcoholic Hallucinosis

More prominent early phase features.
Visual, auditory and tactile hallucinations.
More marked anxiety and psychomotor agitation.
Sensorium clear and still orientated.

Delirium Tremens (Advanced Phase)

Peaks about three days after last drink.
Intense restlessness and agitation.
Tachycardia, hyper- or hypotension, hyperventilation.
Profuse sweating and fever.
Hallucinations – 'horrors'.
Paranoia, confusion, disorientation.
Clouding of consciousness, coma and death.

Medical Complications

Withdrawal Fits

Can occur in any of the above phases. Usually begin within 12 to 48 hours of withdrawal. Can continue up to five days. Usually grand mal type.

Dehydration

Vomiting, fever and sweating.
Hypokalaemia and hyperkalaemia.

Hypoglycaemia or Hyperglycaemia

Hyperventilation with Hypomagnesaemia and Hypocalcaemia

Vitamin Deficiency

Especially thiamine and folate.

Management

At Home

The very mildest case not requiring medication.
Provided there is caring, intelligent supervision and medical
    help if necessary.

In Community Detox Units – 'Social Detoxication'

Personal continuous care with or without drug therapy.
Stress-free environment.
By trained paraprofessionals (often stable, recovered
    alcoholics).
Should be assessed by nurse or doctor as:
    free from acute medical, surgical, psychiatric illness or
    complication;
    unlikely to advance to more severe withdrawal phase.
Immediate referral to hospital if complications develop.
On recovery, referral to:
    alcohol assessment treatment agencies;
    medical assessment.

Up to 75% of patients at the less severe end of the
spectrum can be brought safely through withdrawal by
social detoxication.

In Hospital

This is mandatory for:
    Severe withdrawal symptoms.
    Associated alcohol-induced disease.
    Intercurrent medical, surgical or psychiatric illness.

Hospital Management Includes:

Fastidious and concerned care from experienced nursing
    and medical staff.

Correction of dehydration, hypoglycaemia, hypokalaemia and hypomagnesaemia by appropriate intravenous fluid therapy.

Attention to nutrition and correction of vitamin deficiencies, especially thiamine, and other B vitamins using Parentrovite.

Use of tranquillising, anti-convulsant drugs in the more advanced stages. Weaning off over 2–6 days (see Table on following page).

Note: Tranquillisers and sedatives such as diazepam (Valium) and chlormethiazole (Heminevrin) must not be used on a long-term basis after acute withdrawal. They can be highly addictive in the dependence-prone alcoholic.

Guidelines for Drug Therapy

(A) ALCOHOL WITHDRAWAL SYNDROME

Clinical Picture	Drug	Route	Initial Dose	Interval	Comment
Early–Immediate Phase Alcohol Withdrawal	Chlormethiazole (Heminevrin)	Oral	500–1500 mg, 1–3 caps	q.i.d.	Reduce dose in chronic bronchitis
	or Oxazepam	Oral	10–30 mg	q.i.d.	Shorter action than diazepam
	or Chloral hydrate	Oral	500–1000 mg, 1–2 caps	nocte	For insomnia up to 7 days only
Alcoholic Hallucinosis	Haloperidol (Serenace)	IM	5 mg	stat	1–3 mg b.i.d. maintenance. May
		Oral	3 mg	2–6 hrly	cause hypotension or promote fit
Advanced Phase Withdrawal (Delirium Tremens)	Chlormethiazole (Heminevrin)	IV	50–100 ml, 0.8% soln.	5 mins	Then maintenance 500–1000 ml
		Oral	1500 ml, 3 caps	3–4 hrly	6–12 hrly, or 1–2 caps q.i.d.
	Diazepam (Valium)	IV	2.5–10 mg by infusion and repeat hrly intervals	5 mins	Then maintenance dose 10–20 mg t.i.d.
		Oral	10–20 mg	2–4 hrly	

(B) SEIZURE DISORDER

Clinical Picture	Drug	Route	Initial Dose	Interval	Comment
Previous or Recent Seizure	Phenytoin	IM/IV	250 mg vials (50 mg/min IV)		Loading dose 250–500 mg then
		Oral	300 mg stat		100–200 mg orally t.i.d. for 5 days
	or Sodium Valproate (Epilim)	Oral	600 mg (3 tabs) stat	t.i.d.	Then 400 mg t.i.d. for 5 days
	or Carbamazepine (Tegretol)	Oral	400 mg (2 tabs) stat	t.i.d.	Then 200 mg t.i.d. for 5 days / Avoid nausea and ataxia
Acute Seizure (Status Epilepticus)	Diazepam (Valium)	IV	5–20 mg slowly stat	5 mins	Then as above (as maintenance to prevent further seizures)

(C) VITAMIN DEFICIENCY SYNDROMES

Prevention of Wernicke's Encephalopathy and Korsakoff Psychosis	Parentrovite (Multivitamins and thiamine)	IV	10 ml (2 amps)	stat	Repeat daily for 3 days if evidence of deficiency or malnutrition
		IM	7 ml (2 amps)	stat	Then oral multivitamins 1–3 months

(D) DRUG THERAPY DURING WITHDRAWAL FROM ADDICTIVE PRESCRIPTION DRUGS

Hypnosedative or Barbiturate Withdrawal	Sodium gardenal	IM/IV	200 mg hrly as required (×3) until moderate sedation or signs of intoxication	stat	If necessary supplementary doses may be given for up to 5 days
	Phenobarbitone Oral	Oral	60 mg hrly (200–800 mg total dose)		
Minor Tranquilliser or Benzodiazepine Withdrawal	Diazepam (Valium)	Oral	10 mg hrly (30–90 mg total dose)	stat	Then reduce dose by 10% per day

(E) OTHER COMMON CONDITIONS

Systemic Infection	Antibiotics	IM/ Oral	As indicated		5-day course
Acute Gastritis with Vomiting	Prochlorperazine (Stemetil)	IM	12.5–25 mg	2 hrly	Avoid over-sedation
Hypoglycaemia	Dextrose	IV	20 ml of 50% stat		Then oral glucose drinks and a small meal with thiamine supplements (e.g. Parentrovite)

N.B. * *Exclude* other causes of agitation or confusion prior to initial sedation, e.g. thiamine deficiency, dehydration, subdural haematoma, pneumonia.
  * *Review* regularly, level of consciousness, respiratory and cardiovascular function, and hydration and nutrition prior to further sedation.
  * Psychotropic medication should be withheld if drowsy, or metabolic intolerance present (e.g. serious liver disease).

Medical Problems Associated with Intoxication and Withdrawal

Other drugs.
Hypoglycaemia.
Dehydration.
Electrolyte disturbance.
Metabolic acidosis.
Metabolic alkalosis.
Hyperthermia.
Wernicke's encephalopathy.
Trauma.
Subdural haematoma.
Aspiration pneumonia.
Dysrhythmias.

Medical Problems Related to Alcohol

Gastritis.
Peptic ulcer.
Gastrointestinal haemorrhage.
Pancreatitis.
Malnutrition.
Anaemia.

Alcohol End-organ Disease

Alcohol liver disease.
Fatty liver.
Alcoholic hepatitis.
Alcoholic cirrhosis.
 ± Ascites.
± Portal encephalopathy.
± Varices.
± Hepatorenal syndrome.
Cardiomyopathy.
Korsakoff's psychosis.
Dementia – cerebral atrophy.
Cerebellar degeneration.

Amblyopia.
Peripheral neuropathy.
Myopathy.

Concurrent Medical Problems

Diabetes mellitus.
Epilepsy.
Hypertension.
Myocardial infarction.
Chronic obstructive lung disease.
Pneumonia.
Sepsis.
Tuberculosis.
Other unrelated systemic diseases, e.g. haemopoietic, carcinoma, gastrointestinal, muscles, bones, joints, neurological.

Indications for Hospitalisation

Presence of medical or surgical condition requiring treatment, e.g. hepatic decompensation, infection, dehydration, haemorrhage, malnutrition, cardiovascular collapse, cardiac arrhythmias, trauma, acute pancreatitis, uncontrolled diabetes.
Hallucinations, tachycardia >110 per minute, severe tremor, extreme agitation or history of severe withdrawal symptoms.
Fever > 38.5° C.
Ataxia, nystagmus, internuclear ophthalmoplegia (Wernicke's encephalopathy).
Confusion or delirium.
Seizures: generalised seizure occurring for the first time in the withdrawal state, focal seizures, status epilepticus, seizures in patients withdrawing from a combination of alcohol and other drugs.
Recent history of head injury with loss of consciousness.
Social isolation, severe depression, or psychiatric illness.

Long-term Management and Rehabilitation

The goals of treatment are:

1. To assist the alcoholic to acknowledge his problem is related to alcohol.
2. To direct the alcoholic in altering his destructive lifestyle, using either behavioural or biomedical assistance.
3. To support the alcoholic in developing and maintaining the improved state of well-being following alcohol withdrawal.

Long-term management involves two strategies:

1. *That aimed at altering the drinking pattern* of a person, e.g. achieving abstinence in the alcohol dependence syndrome. This involves education, motivation, personal and family counselling, behaviour modification on either an inpatient or outpatient basis.
2. *That aimed at dealing with related problems*, other than drinking, either physical or emotional, social, spiritual or legal. This will depend on an accurate initial assessment and continued monitoring of a person's health and other needs.

Regular review, at least on a monthly basis for the first six months and thereafter every three months for two years, is essential in most cases.

Long-term management necessitates use of all available resources, including Alcoholics Anonymous, nursing services, general practitioners, social workers, local alcoholism agencies and hospital units; also individual treatment units which may provide outpatient family care, psychotherapy or specific behavioural techniques, relaxation, physical and occupational therapy. A team approach is essential for more advanced cases.

For *more intensive care*, specialist programmes are available on an inpatient or an intensive outpatient basis in most major cities. Indications include major, chronic alcohol-related illnesses or disabilities, severe fragmentation of family and friends, or an inadequately supportive social environment.

Even after discharge from such programmes, alcoholics will still need *intensive follow-up*, either by the programme staff or by the general practitioner, with or without the support of disulfiram (Antabuse), Alcoholics Anonymous, and Al-Anon for the family.

A person with a well-developed alcohol dependence syndrome cannot recover from his illness by simply having a minor tranquilliser or sedative prescribed; and chlormethiazole, in particular, should be reserved for specialised clinics to be used in the withdrawal of patients only, in a supervised setting and for no more than five days without review.

Long-term management, after intensive therapy, may include the prescribing of tricyclic antidepressants or major tranquillisers, if indicated following psychiatric assessment. These medications are ineffective and dangerous if used with alcohol.

Prolonged vitamin therapy is unnecessary in most cases, but supplements of both minerals and particularly B-complex and folic acid vitamins are helpful for several months after alcohol withdrawal, together with nutritional counselling.

Disulfiram (Antabuse)

Mode of Action

Inhibits hepatic transformation of alcohol's first metabolite, acetaldehyde, to acetate by the enzyme acetaldehyde dehydrogenase.

Alcohol ingestion causes accumulation of acetaldehyde and a resulting toxic reaction.

The Disulfiram—Alcohol Reaction

5—15 minutes after ingestion.
Flushing, tachycardia, nausea, anxiety.
More severe – vomiting, dyspnoea, hypotension.
Supportive treatment. No specific antidote.
Usually over in an hour or more.

Indications and Requirements

Alcohol dependence.
Absence of severe hepatic, renal or cardiac insufficiency.
No significant brain damage.
Absence of serious depression or psychoses.
Stable social support.
Co-operative patient understanding the therapy and the
significance of the reaction with alcohol.
Continued counselling support.

Dosage

400 mg daily for three days then 100—200 mg in water
daily at night to avoid drowsiness;
or
400—800 mg twice weekly.

Effects persist from 4—7 days from last dose.

Side Effects

Are uncommon with lower doses now used.
Minor – drowsiness, fatigue, metallic taste.
Major, occur rarely – drug rash, impotence, confusion,
hepatotoxicity, neuropathy.

Drug Interactions

With isoniazid, phenytoin, warfarin.

Rationale

Originally seen as a form of conditioned aversive treatment. Now seen as a symbol of co-operation and a protection against impulsive use of alcohol.

May need a course of 6–12 months or more before it can be replaced by 'internal controls' developed during rehabilitative therapy.

Alcoholics Anonymous (AA)

Is a self-help group for the support and rehabilitation of dependent alcoholics.

Is the first self-help group in modern times – established 1935.

Has the largest membership of over one million members in over 110 mainly western countries.

It is difficult to obtain objective data, but it appears at present to be the single most powerful force in bringing dependent alcoholics to permanent contented sobriety.

The AA philosophy and organisation is summed up in the 'Twelve Steps' and the 'Twelve Traditions'.

The Twelve Steps

1. We admitted we were powerless over alcohol – that our lives had become unmanageable.
2. Came to believe that a Power greater than ourselves could restore us to sanity.
3. Made a decision to turn our will and our lives over to the care of God *as we understand Him.*
4. Made a searching and fearless moral inventory of ourselves.
5. Admitted to God, to ourselves, and to another human being the exact nature of our wrongs.
6. Were entirely ready to have God remove all these defects of character.
7. Humbly asked Him to remove our shortcomings.
8. Made a list of all persons we had harmed, and became willing to make amends to them all.
9. Made direct amends to such people wherever possible, except when to do so would injure them or others.

10. Continued to take personal inventory and when we were wrong promptly admitted it.
11. Sought through prayer and meditation to improve our conscious contact with God *as we understood Him*, praying only for knowledge of His will for us and the power to carry that out.
12. Having had a spiritual awakening as the result of these steps, we tried to carry this message to alcoholics and to practise these principles in all our affairs.

Note: In this context God means a 'Higher Power' and need not have a particular religious or Christian connotation.

The Twelve Traditions

1. Our common welfare should come first; personal recovery depends upon AA unity.
2. For our group purpose there is but one ultimate authority – a loving God as He may express Himself in our group conscience. Our leaders are but trusted servants; they do not govern.
3. The only requirement for AA membership is a desire to stop drinking.
4. Each group should be autonomous except in matters affecting other groups or AA as a whole.
5. Each group has but one primary purpose – to carry its message to the alcoholic who still suffers.
6. An AA group ought never endorse, finance, or lend the AA name to any related facility or outside enterprise, lest problems of money, property, and prestige divert us from our primary purpose.
7. Every AA group ought to be fully self-supporting, declining outside contributions.
8. Alcoholics Anonymous should remain forever non-professional, but our service centres may employ special workers.

9. Alcoholics Anonymous, as such, ought never be organised; but we may create service boards or committees directly responsible to those they serve.
10. Alcoholics Anonymous has no opinion on outside issues; hence the AA name ought never be drawn into public controversy.
11. Our public relations policy is based on attraction rather than promotion; we need always to maintain personal anonymity at the level of press, radio and film.
12. Anonymity is the spiritual foundation of all our traditions, ever reminding us to place principles before personalities.

The Twelve Steps and Twelve Traditions reprinted with permission of AA World Services, Inc., New York, USA.

Health Workers Need to Understand and Co-operate with AA by:

Attending open meetings from time to time (the best way of beginning to understand the alcoholic).

Making contact with local AA members who are skilled in the 'Twelfth Step' or experienced sponsors.

Using every possible means to bring the dependent alcoholic to AA membership.

Al-Anon and Alateen

Are allied organisations which support the spouses and families of drinking and recovering dependent alcoholics. Health workers can alleviate the secondary damage in the alcoholic's family by referring individuals to these groups for education and support.

If they cannot make contact with the alcoholic, referral of the spouse or family to Al-Anon or Alateen may be the only constructive alternative.

Women and Alcohol

Traditionally, compliance has been inculcated in women in the home, educational institutions and the workplace.

Although there is increasing evidence to support women's changing role in society, the double standards and stigmas die hard and those surrounding women and alcohol are no exception.

It is considered more degrading for a woman to be drunk than it is for a man.

The alcoholic female is labelled a 'fallen woman' and is often considered promiscuous.

It is acceptable for men to use alcohol to cope with stress. It seems more acceptable for women to use mood-altering prescription medicines.

Employers fire a male alcoholic or pressure him to seek treatment; women are more often ignored, then given leave of absence before being let go.

Police officers pick up an intoxicated man, charge him, jail him, or take him to a 'detox' centre. A woman is more likely to be protected because she is both intoxicated and a woman. She is usually released and sent home in the care of relatives or friends.

There are many factors involved in women's abuse of alcohol and other drugs, some unique to women, others common to both sexes:

Disintegration of traditional roles.
Boredom, loneliness, anger, frustration, lack of self-worth.
Coping with stress in the work environment.
Marital difficulties, separation, divorce, bereavement.
Coping with societal attitudes towards women.
The 'empty nest' syndrome, and isolation in the home.
Physical problems related to women's cyclic body chemistry.
Pressure in competing with men for equal opportunities.

Female Drinking Patterns

Current trends indicate that:

More women are consuming more alcohol.
Drinking is beginning at an earlier age.
More women are drinking in public.
The male preponderance in alcoholism is gradually diminishing.

The Female Alcoholic

Has been the subject of only limited research but has many of the same characteristics as the male alcoholic. Some differences include:

More secret drinking and social isolation.
Tendency to stronger denial and later detection.
More progressive downhill course once dependence occurs.
A vulnerability to physical complications, especially liver disease.
More frequent association with prescription drug abuse.
Higher incidence of separation or desertion by spouse.
Higher incidence of associated affective disorders.

The Alcoholic Doctor

Importance

Concern for a suffering colleague and his family.

Concern for the hazards to patients.

Concern for the public image of the profession and its capability for self-regulation.

Incidence

Along with drug abuse, accounts for about 70% of sick or impaired doctors.

Hard facts are scarce.

Drug abuse is many times commoner among doctors than in the general population.

Alcoholism occurs at least as often as in the general population; there is a suspicion there may be a higher than average incidence.

Characteristics of the Alcoholic Doctor

Represented proportionately in all branches of medicine.

Pre-morbid academic ability is comparable to the non-alcoholic.

In 50% of cases, has poly-drug abuse.

Presents late with social, professional and legal complications.

Often shows strong denial and reluctance to accept treatment.

Is often 'covered-up' by family and colleagues.

Professional intervention has been uncommon or late and ineffective.

Prevention

More emphasis in undergraduate and postgraduate education on addiction, unhealthy lifestyles, and ways of handling stress.

Early Detection, Treatment and Rehabilitation

Following successful experience in North America, consideration is now being given to the establishment of 'Sick Doctor' committees in other countries.

In North American programmes, the committees have:

Been small, three or four, with some members from outside the district.

Included recovered alcoholic doctors and others skilled in the alcoholism field, particularly in the technique of confrontation.

Been confidential, kept no records, and made no reports to or contacts with the medical association or licensing body.

Conducted an educational campaign about the problem among doctors, their families and the public, encouraging anonymous and confidential reporting of impaired doctors to the committee.

If there is good evidence of an alcohol or drug problem, sent two or more members to visit the impaired doctor and if possible the spouse.

Used the confrontation technique described in this handbook.

Always acted with caring concern for the suffering doctor, using therapeutic coercion rather than the threat of deregistration to persuade him to enter a treatment programme.

Offered help and support in finding a treatment facility, obtaining a locum and sickness insurance, etc.

If intervention is unsuccessful, offered immediate assistance if it is needed at any time in the future, and warned that any further complaint would be passed directly to the disciplinary or registering body.

Experience in North America suggests that:

Unfounded or malicious complaints were rare.
Resort to deregistration was uncommon.
Many more doctors were accepting treatment.
Rehabilitation of doctors was as effective as of other groups.

Prevention

Prevention

Alcoholism is a major and increasing community health problem. Individual health workers have a duty to promote effective preventive measures.

Primary Prevention

Health and social problems resulting from alcohol use are directly related to the per capita consumption in the community. Consumption has increased steadily over the last 25 years in all industrialised societies. Health workers should consider supporting measures that might lower consumption. These include the following.

Social Controls

Opposing lowering of the legal drinking age.
Opposing further liberalisation of licensing hours, or increase in the number of liquor outlets.
Supporting higher taxation (and increased real cost of liquor), based on its alcohol content.
Supporting the removal of alcoholic liquor from the cost of living index.
Supporting the introduction of low alcohol-content beers and wines.
Supporting a ban on all alcohol advertising and associated sports and cultural promotion.

Personal Example

Encouraging moderation by:
   Personal example.
   Promoting drink-free days.
   Promoting occasional drink-free social occasions.
   Supporting measures to discourage drink/driving.

Educational Strategies

Supporting valid and proven educational programmes in schools, in the media and in the family.

Supporting adequate alcohol study courses and alcohol related research in medical and other health professional schools.

Supporting voluntary and government agencies.

Supporting mental health and other programmes and activities which promote drug-free ways of coping with stress.

Secondary Prevention

Early detection and treatment of hazardous and problem drinkers in clinical practice.

Advising the pregnant woman about alcohol.

Counselling children of alcoholic parents about their own vulnerability.

Counselling clients coping with significant life events about the risks of excessive drinking.

Support and occasional attendance at meetings of AA, Al-Anon and Alateen.

Encouragement and co-operation with 'Alcohol in Industry' programmes.

Encouragement and co-operation with drink/driver programmes.

Appendices

Appendix 1:
Alcoholism Questionnaires

CAGE Test (Mayfield *et al.*, 1974)

1. Have you ever felt you should *cut* down on your drinking?
2. Have people *annoyed* you by criticising your drinking?
3. Have you ever felt bad or *guilty* about your drinking?
4. Have you ever had a drink first thing in the morning to steady your nerves or get rid of a hang-over? (*Eye-opener*)

Two or three positive responses suggest alcohol dependence.

Brief MAST (Pokorny *et al.*, 1972)

Circle correct answer

Do you feel you are a normal drinker?	YES	NO (2 pts)
Do friends or relatives think you are a normal drinker? ...	YES	NO (2 pts)
Have you ever attended a meeting of Alcoholics Anonymous? ...	YES (5 pts)	NO
Have you ever lost friends or girlfriends or boyfriends because of drinking?	YES (2 pts)	NO
Have you ever got into trouble at work because of drinking?	YES (2 pts)	NO
Have you ever neglected your obligations, your family, or your work for two or more days in a row because you were drinking?	YES (2 pts)	NO

contd.

Have you ever had delirium
    tremens (DTs), severe shaking,
    heard voices or seen things
    that were not there after heavy
    drinking?   ...   . YES (5 pts)   NO

Have you ever gone to anyone for
    help about your drinking?   ... YES (5 pts)   NO

Have you ever been in a hospital
    because of drinking?   ...   ... YES (5 pts)   NO

Have you ever been arrested for
    drunken driving or driving
    after drinking?   ...   ... YES (2 pts)   NO

Total score

Five or more points said to be diagnostic.

Elura Test

	Score
Previous convictions for drunkenness?	3
History of blackouts after drinking?	2
Have you ever felt guilty about drinking?	2
Health affected detrimentally?	1
'Drinking speeds up life for me.'	4
'My family think I drink too much.'	1
'I go on a weekend binge now and then.'	3
Do you feel you are a normal drinker (no)?	2
Have you ever lost a job because of drinking?	2
Work competence impaired?	1
History of drug dependence in family (present)?	3

Total score

If a total score is above six, alcohol dependence is likely.

Appendix 2:
Principal Agencies Concerned with Alcoholism in the UK, New Zealand and Australia

UK

Alcoholics Anonymous (AA). Number in telephone directory.

Al-Anon and Alateen. Branches of AA devoted respectively to spouses and teenage children of alcoholics.

Alcoholism Community Centre for Education, Prevention and Treatment (ACCEPT). Address: Western Hospital, Seagrave Road, London SW16 1RZ. Tel: 01-381 3155.

Alcohol Concern. Address: 3 Grosvenor Crescent, London SW1 6LD. Tel: 01-235 4182.

Scottish Council on Alcoholism. Address: 147 Blythswood Street, Glasgow G2 4EN. Tel: 041-333 9677.

Northern Ireland Council on Alcoholism. Address: 36–40 Victoria Square, Belfast 1. Tel: 0232 38173/38202.

Local Councils on Alcoholism. Number in telephone directory.

Medical Council on Alcoholism. Address: 31 Bedford Square, London WC1B 3JS. Tel: 01-580 3893.

Alcohol Education and Research Council. Address: Whittington House, 19–30 Alfred Place, London WC1E 7EJ.

New Zealand

Most agencies concerned with alcoholism in New Zealand can be found in the *Directory of Treatment Facilities for Alcoholism in New Zealand*. This is published by The Alcoholic Liquor Advisory Council, and is now in its third edition. Further information relating to the agencies listed below can be found in the directory.

The Alcoholic Liquor Advisory Council, PO Box 5023, Wellington. Tel: 720-997.

Alcoholics Anonymous (AA). General Service Office: Box 6458, Wellington. Tel: 859-455.

Al-Anon and Alateen. Information Service: PO Box 39–373, Auckland West *or* PO Box 2148, Christchurch.

National Society on Alcoholism and Drug Dependence: Centres in Wellington, Waimate, Hamilton, Tokoroa, Tauranga, Auckland.

Salvation Army Bridge Programme, PO Box 6033, Te Aro, 31 Vivian Street, Wellington 1. Tel: 859-233, 859-200.

Australia

As for New Zealand, most of the agencies concerned with alcoholism in Australia can be found in one directory. This is published by the Australian Foundation on Alcoholism and Drug Dependence (AFADD). The address of this organisation is given below, along with a representative list of alcoholism-related agencies for Australia. Finally, *Australians and Alcoholism* (1976) by P. Davis and published by Paul Hamlyn gives an extensive list of agencies concerned with alcoholism in Australia.

Australian Foundation of Alcoholism and Drug Dependence (AFADD), 2nd Fl, T & G Bldg, London Circuit, Canberra City, ACT 2601 *or* PO Box 477, Canberra City, ACT 2601. Tel: (062)47 3939.

Alcoholics Anonymous (AA). Offices in all states and most major cities.

Western Australian Alcohol and Drug Dependence Industrial Committee, 19 Irwin St, Perth, WA 6000. Tel: (09)325 3566.

Darwin and District Alcohol and Drug Dependence Federation, Amity House, 79 Cavenagh St, Darwin, NT 5790 *or* PO Box 5360, Darwin, NT 5794. Tel: 81 8030.

South Australian Foundation on Alcoholism and Drug Dependence, 84 Archer St, North Adelaide 5086. Tel: 267 2187.

Victorian Foundation on Alcoholism and Drug Dependence, 153 Park St, South Melbourne, Vic 3000. Tel: (03)690 6000.

Foundation for Research and Treatment of Alcoholism and Drug Dependence of NSW, 37 Macpherson St, Mosman, NSW 2088. Tel: 90 6279.

Alcohol and Drug Problems Association of Queensland, 129 Leichhardt St, Brisbane, Qld 4000 *or* PO Box 320, North Brisbane, Qld 4000.

Tasmanian Foundation on Alcoholism and Drug Dependence, John Edis Hospital, Creek Rd, New Town, Tas. 7008 *or* PO Box 114, Moonah, Tas. 7009. Tel: 28 8351.

National Committee for the Prevention of Alcoholism, 148 Fox Valley Rd, Wahroonga, NSW 2067. Tel: (02)48 1061.

Appendix 3:
Bibliography on Alcohol and Alcoholism

Books

Addiction Research Foundation (1978). *Antabuse (Disulfiram) in the Treatment of Alcoholism*. ARF Ontario, Canada.

Alcohol and Drug Dependence Clinic, Memphis Technical Institute and University of Tennessee Centre for the Health Sciences (1977). *Physician's role in the diagnosis and treatment of alcoholism and alcohol-related disorders*, 5 vols. Southern Area Alcohol Education and Training Programme.

Alcohol Problems. (1982). Articles from the British Medical Journal. British Medical Association.

Armyr G., Elmér A., Herz U. (1982). *Alcohol in the World of the 80s. Habits, Attitudes, Preventive Policies and Voluntary Efforts*. Stockholm: Sober Förlags.

Corrigan E. M. (1980). *Alcoholic Women in Treatment*. Oxford: Oxford University Press.

Edwards G. *et al.*, eds. (1977). *Alcohol-related Disabilities*. Geneva: World Health Organisation.

Edwards G., Grant M., eds. (1977). *Alcoholism – New Knowledge and New Responses*. London: Croom Helm.

Fisher M. M., Rankin J. G., eds. (1977). *Alcohol and the Liver*. London: Plenum.

Forrest G. G. (1978). *The Diagnosis and Treatment of Alcoholism*, 2nd edn. Springfield: Charles C. Thomas.

Jacobson G. R. (1976). *The Alcoholisms; Detection, Assessment and Diagnosis*. Human Sciences Press.

Jellinek E. M. (1960). *The Disease Concept of Alcoholism*. College and University Press.

Kissin B., Begleiter H., eds. (1971–1977). *The Biology of Alcoholism*, 5 vols. London: Plenum.

Kricka L., Clark P. (1979). *Biochemistry of Alcohol and Alcoholism*. New York: John Wiley & Sons.

Lieber C. S., ed. (1977). *Metabolic Aspects of Alcoholism*. Lancaster: MTP Press.

Madden J. S., Walker R., Kenyon W. H., eds. (1977). *Alcoholism and Drug Dependence; A Multidisciplinary Approach.* London: Plenum.

Orford J., Edwards G. (1977). *Alcoholism; A Comparison of Treatment and Advice with a Study of the Influence of Marriage.* Oxford: Oxford University Press.

Research Advances in Alcohol and Drug Problems. Wiley (Vols. 1 to 3), Plenum (Vol. 4–).

Richter D., ed. (1980). *Addiction and Brain Damage.* London: Croom Helm.

Rix J. B., Rix E. (1983). *Alcohol Problems.* Bristol: Wright.

Royal College of Psychiatrists (1979). *Report of Special Committee on Alcohol and Alcoholism.* London: Tavistock Publications.

Seixas F. A. (1977). *Currents in Alcoholism*, Vol. 1. London: Grune and Stratton.

Seixas F. A., Williams K., Eggleston S., eds. (1975). *Medical Consequences of Alcoholism.* Ann. New York Acad. Sci. Vol. 252.

Seixas F. A., Eggleston S., eds. (1976). *Work in Progress on Alcoholism.* Ann. New York Acad. Sci. Vol. 273.

Sobell M., Sobell L. (1980). *Behavioural Treatment of Alcohol Problems.* London: Plenum.

Tarter R. E., Sugermann A. A., eds. (1976). *Alcoholism: Interdisciplinary Approaches to an Enduring Problem.* London: Addison-Wesley.

Taylor D. (1981). *Alcohol: Reducing the Harm.* London: Office of Health Economics.

Victor M., Adams R. D., Collins G. H. (1971). *Wernicke-Korsakoff Syndrome: A Clinical and Pathological Study of 245 Patients, 82 with Post-mortem Examinations.* Contemporary Neurology Series, 7. Philadelphia: Davis.

Wilkins R. H. (1974). *The Hidden Alcoholic in General Practice.* Paul Elek (Scientific Books) Ltd.

Wilson P. (1980). *Drinking in England and Wales. A Survey by the OPCS.* London: HMSO.

Zimberg S., Wallace J., Blume S. B., eds. (1978). *Practical Approaches to Alcoholism Psychotherapy.* London: Plenum.

Journal Articles

Medical Complications

Abbasakoor A., Beanlands D. S., Macleod S. M. (1976). Electrocardiographic changes during ethanol withdrawal. *Ann. New York Acad. Sci;* **273**: 364–70.

Abel E. L. (1980). A review of alcohol's effects on sex and reproduction. *Drug and Alcohol Dependence;* **5**: 321–2.

Anderson M. (1978). Treatment in an alcoholism and drug addiction unit. *N.Z. Med. J;* **88**: 233–7.

Ashley M. J., Rankin J. G. (1979). Alcohol consumption and hypertension: the evidence from hazardous drinking and alcoholic populations. *Aust. N.Z.J. Med;* **9**: 201–206.

Ashley M. J., Rankin J. G. (1980). Hazardous alcohol consumption and diseases of the circulatory system. *J. Stud. Alc;* **41**: 1040–70.

Ashley M. J. (1981). Alcohol use during pregnancy: a challenge for the 80's (Symposium). *Canad. Med. Ass. J;* **125**: 141.

Ashley M. J., LeRich W. H., Kornaczewski A., Schmitt W., Rankin J. G. (1976). Skid row alcoholism. *Arch. Intern. Med;* **136**: 272–8.

Bagjurst K. I. (1980). Nutritional and health aspects of alcohol consumption. *Med. J. Aust;* **2**: 177–80.

Bhatal P. S., Wilkinson P., Clifton S., Rankin J. G., Santamaria J. N. (1975). The spectrum of liver disease in alcoholism. *Aust. N.Z. J. Med;* **5**: 49–57.

Bjorkholm M. (1980). Immunological and haematological abnormalities in chronic alcoholism. *Acta Med. Scand;* **207**: 197–200.

Cala L. A., Janes B., Mastaglia F. L., Wiley B. (1978). Brain atrophy and intellectual impairment in heavy drinkers – A clinical, psychometric and computerized tomography study. *Aust. N.Z. J. Med;* **8**: 147–53.

Carlen P. L., Wilkinson D. A., Wortzman G., Holgate R., Cordingley J., Lee M. A., Huszer L., Moddel G., Singh R., Kiraly L., Rankin J. G. (1981). Cerebral atrophy and functional deficits in alcoholics without clinically apparent liver disease. *Neurology;* **31**: 377–85.

Collins E. (1980). Alcohol in pregnancy. *Med. J. Aust;* **2**: 173–5.

Cutting J. (1978). The relationship between Korsakoff's syndrome and alcoholic dementia. *Brit. J. Psych;* **132**: 240–51.

Cutting J. (1978). Specific psychological deficits in alcoholism. *Brit. J. Psych;* **133**: 199–222.

Dalen N., Lambe B. (1976). Bone mineral losses in alcoholics. *Acta Orthop. Scand;* **47**: 469–71.

Duncan G., Lambie D., Johnson R. H., Whiteside E. A. (1980). Evidence of vagal neuropathy in chronic alcoholics. *Lancet;* **2**: 1053–7.

Eckardt M. J. *et al.* (1978). Relationship between neuro-psychological performance and alcohol consumption in alcoholics. *Biol. Psych;* **13**: 551–65.

Fetal-Alcohol Syndrome: A Symposium. (1980). *Alcoholism: Clin. Exp. Research;* **4**.

Galbraith S., Murray W. R., Patel A. R., Knill-Jones R. (1976). The relationship between alcohol and head injury and its effect on the conscious level. *Brit. J. Surg;* **63**: 128–30.

Isselbacher K. J. (1977). Metabolic and hepatic effects of alcohol. *New Eng. J. Med;* **296**: 612–16.

Kallas P., Sellers E. M. (1975). Blood glucose in intoxicated chronic alcoholics. *Canad. Med. Ass. J;* **112**: 590–1.

Kitson T. M., Bieder L. (1977). Drugs which interfere with alcohol metabolism. *N.Z. Med. J;* **86**: 135–7.

Levi G. F., Quadri A., Ratti S., Basagni M. (1977). Pre-clinical abnormality of left ventricular function in chronic alcoholics. *Brit. Heart J;* **39**: 35–7.

Parsons D. A. (1980). Cognitive dysfunction in alcoholics and social drinkers – Problems in assessment and remediation. *J. Stud. Alc;* **41**: 105–18.

Pequignot G., Tuyns A. J., Berta J. L. (1978). Ascitic cirrhosis in relation to alcohol consumption. *Internat. J. Epidem;* **7**: 113–20.

Seixas F. A., ed. (1977). The metabolism of alcohol: a seminar. *Alcoholism: Clin. Exp. Research;* **1**: 5–50.

Smith D. W., Jones K. L. (1973). Recognition of the fetal alcohol syndrome in early infancy. *Lancet;* **2**: 999–1001.

Tarter R. E. (1975). Psychological deficit in chronic alcoholics. *Internat. J. Add;* **10**: 327–58.

Van Thiel D. H., Lester R. (1976). Alcoholism: its effects on hypothalamic, pituitary, gonadal function. *Gastroenterology;* **71**: 318–27.

Whitfield J. B. (1981). Alcohol related biochemical changes in heavy drinkers. *Aust. N.Z. J. Med;* **11**: 132–9.

Diagnosis

Barrison I. G., Viola L., Murray-Lyon I. M. (1980). Do Housemen take an adequate drinking history? *Brit. Med. J;* **281**: 1040.

Chick J. *et al.* (1981). MCV and serum enzyme as markers for alcoholics. *Lancet;* **1**: 1251–9.

Editorial (1980). Screening tests for alcoholism? *Lancet;* **2**: 1117–18.

Hore B. D., Wilkins R. H. (1976). A general-practice study of the commonest presenting symptoms of alcoholism. *J. R.C.G.P;* **26**: 140–2.

Mayfield D., McLeod G., Hale P. (1974). The CAGE questionnaire. *Am. J. Psych;* **131**: 1121–3.

National Council on Alcoholism. (1972). Criteria for the diagnosis of alcoholism. *Amer. J. Psych;* **129**: 2.

Pokorny A. D., Miller B. A., Kaplan H. B. (1972). The Brief MAST: a shortened version of the Michigan Alcoholism Screening Test; *Amer. J. Psych;* **129**: 342–5.

Sellers E. M. (1976). Alcohol and organic disease: calculation of consumption. *Canad. Med. Ass. J;* 114.

Selzer M. L., Winokur A., Van Rooijen L. A. (1975). Self-administered short Michigan alcoholism screening test (SMAST). *J. Stud. Alc;* **36**: 117–26.

Skinner H. A., Holt S., Israel Y. (1981). Early identification of alcohol abuse. 1. Critical issues and psychosocial indicators for a composite index. *Canad. Med. Ass. J;* **124**: 1141–52.

Skinner H. A., Holt S., Israel Y. (1981). Early identification of alcohol abuse. 2. Clinical and laboratory indicators. *Canad. Med. Ass. J;* **124**: 1279–99.

Management

Kulik F., Wilbur R. (1981). Detoxification of alcoholics with drugs: perspectives in treatment and research. *Health and Research World;* 50–4.

Martin P. R., Bhushan M. K., Whiteside E. A., Sellers E. M. (1979). Intravenous phenobarbital therapy in barbiturate and other hypnosedative withdrawal reactions: a kinetic approach. *Clin. Pharmacol. Ther;* **26**: 256–64.

Murray R. (1976). The characteristics and prognosis of alcoholic doctors. *Brit. Med. J;* **4**: 1537.

Petursson H., Lader M. H. (1981). Withdrawal from long-term benzodiazepine treatment. *Brit. Med. J;* **283**: 643–5.

Sellers E. M., Kalant H. (1976). Alcohol intoxication and withdrawal. *New Eng. J. Med;* **294**: 757–62.

Smith R. (1981). Alcohol, women and the young. *Brit. Med. J;* **283**: 1170–4.

Smith R. (1981). Preventing alcohol problems: a job for Canute? *Brit. Med. J;* **283**: 972–5.

Index